Original title:
A Symphony of Aspiring Smiles

Copyright © 2025 Swan Charm
All rights reserved.

Author: Kätriin Kaldaru
ISBN HARDBACK: 978-9908-1-3166-5
ISBN PAPERBACK: 978-9908-1-3167-2
ISBN EBOOK: 978-9908-1-3168-9

A Tonic of Rising Smiles

A breeze whispers softly, light and free,
Joy dances in shadows, embracing me.
Sunrise paints the sky with hues so bright,
Each moment a blessing, pure delight.

Laughter bounces off the walls of time,
Together we climb, hearts in perfect rhyme.
The world holds wonders, a feast for the eyes,
In every encounter, a sweet surprise.

Gentle dreams float on the edge of night,
With stars as our guide, we'll take to flight.
Hand in hand, we wander, souls entwined,
A tapestry woven, love unconfined.

The echoes of friendship ring clear and true,
In shared stories written anew.
Each smile a tonic, lifting us high,
Revealing the beauty as moments pass by.

So let laughter linger, a gift we share,
In the warmth of connection, we find our care.
With hearts wide open, let kindness flow,
In this tonic of smiles, together we grow.

Tune of Hopeful Horizons

In the dawn's gentle light,
We chase shadows away.
Each step whispers softly,
A promise of a new day.

With every fleeting breeze,
Dreams rise like the sun.
Colors blend in harmony,
Together we have won.

Laughter dances on air,
With hearts wide and free.
Hope blooms in the silence,
Like flowers on a tree.

Through valleys deep and wide,
We venture hand in hand.
Together we'll find strength,
In this ever-changing land.

So let the music play,
On paths yet to unfold.
With the tune of hope,
Our story will be told.

Crescendo of Blossoming Hearts

In the garden of our dreams,
Love begins to grow.
Each petal tells a story,
That only we could know.

With fingers intertwined,
We sway beneath the stars.
Our laughter paints the night,
And heals the deepest scars.

Moments turn to music,
As harmony takes flight.
The melody of candles,
Illuminate the night.

In the rhythm of our hearts,
A symphony is born.
Each note a gentle whisper,
That signals every dawn.

So let the world stand still,
As we dance to our tune.
Two souls in sweet elation,
Swaying under the moon.

Radiant Chords of Contentment

In the quiet of the morn,
Contentment starts to rise.
Sunshine spills through the trees,
Painting warmth in the skies.

With every gentle heartbeat,
Peace wraps us like a shawl.
Together we find solace,
As the world begins to call.

With laughter shared like treasures,
We cherish moments small.
The simplest of connections,
Can mean the most of all.

With radiant chords around us,
Harmony flows true.
In every breath, we find grace,
In all that we pursue.

So let us weave our stories,
With threads of joy and cheer.
In this symphony of living,
Together, we are here.

Dance of Future Dreams

In twilight's gentle glow,
Our dreams begin to rise.
Like stars upon the water,
Reflecting in our eyes.

We twirl through countless wishes,
On paths yet to explore.
With every step we take,
We find ourselves wanting more.

A waltz through life's uncertainties,
With hope as our guide.
Together we will wander,
Side by side, collide.

With every song that beckons,
We dance into the light.
Creating our tomorrow,
With each heartbeat, so bright.

So let the music linger,
In tempo with our dreams.
In this dance of future hopes,
We realize what it means.

Symphony of Cheerful Visions

In the morning light we rise,
With laughter bright beneath the skies.
Colors dance in every heart,
A symphony that won't depart.

Whispers of joy fill the air,
Every moment, sweet and rare.
Joyful melodies intertwine,
Creating dreams that brightly shine.

Gentle breezes, soft and sweet,
Carry our hopes on light feet.
In harmony, we find our way,
Together, we embrace the day.

With every glance, a world anew,
Bright horizons, endless view.
Symphony played in joyous tones,
In the midst, our love has grown.

So let us laugh, and let us sing,
Spread the joy that love can bring.
In cheerful visions, we will bask,
A perfect life, a simple task.

Vibrations of Enthusiastic Spirits

In the dance of lively grace,
Every heartbeat finds its place.
Voices rise like waves in flight,
Vibrations lifting hearts in light.

Through the laughter, warmth expands,
Join together, holding hands.
In the rhythm, we take part,
Enthusiasm fills the heart.

Moments sparkle, spirits soar,
With each hug, we want more.
Energy flows through the crowd,
Bringing joy, so bright, so loud.

Every glance, a spark ignites,
In our souls, enthusiastic lights.
A chorus of vibrant delight,
Chasing shadows, holding tight.

So let the music guide us near,
Every note and echo clear.
In this dance, we truly see,
The power of harmony.

Bursting forth with Silent Joy

In quietude, the laughter grows,
Amidst the stillness, beauty flows.
Silent whispers, secrets shared,
In each moment, love declared.

The hearts entwined, a sacred place,
Bursting forth with gentle grace.
Joy concealed in every smile,
Unspoken truths that last a while.

Colors bloom in muted tones,
Creating worlds in hushed undertones.
Every heartbeat, a soft sigh,
In silent joy, we learn to fly.

So let us savor this sweet pause,
Life's small wonders, gentle cause.
In the stillness, we find our way,
Bursting forth in quiet play.

Together we weave a tapestry,
Of unvoiced joy, a simple plea.
In the silence, hearts rejoice,
In our stillness, we find our voice.

Rhapsody of Grinning Horizons

Beneath the sky, horizons gleam,
A rhapsody that flows like dream.
With every dawn, the world awakes,
Grinning brightly, joy that makes.

Colors splash in radiant hues,
Every moment a joyful muse.
Life is painted, bold and bright,
As we dance in morning light.

With open arms, we greet the day,
Chasing clouds, we laugh and play.
Horizons stretch, our spirits fly,
Underneath this vast, blue sky.

Every journey starts with cheer,
In our hearts, the path is clear.
Grinning wide, we take each chance,
Rhapsody sings, we join the dance.

So let the world embrace our song,
In the melody, we all belong.
With laughter echoing afar,
Grinning horizons, our guiding star.

Bursting forth with Silent Joy

In quietude, the laughter grows,
Amidst the stillness, beauty flows.
Silent whispers, secrets shared,
In each moment, love declared.

The hearts entwined, a sacred place,
Bursting forth with gentle grace.
Joy concealed in every smile,
Unspoken truths that last a while.

Colors bloom in muted tones,
Creating worlds in hushed undertones.
Every heartbeat, a soft sigh,
In silent joy, we learn to fly.

So let us savor this sweet pause,
Life's small wonders, gentle cause.
In the stillness, we find our way,
Bursting forth in quiet play.

Together we weave a tapestry,
Of unvoiced joy, a simple plea.
In the silence, hearts rejoice,
In our stillness, we find our voice.

Rhapsody of Grinning Horizons

Beneath the sky, horizons gleam,
A rhapsody that flows like dream.
With every dawn, the world awakes,
Grinning brightly, joy that makes.

Colors splash in radiant hues,
Every moment a joyful muse.
Life is painted, bold and bright,
As we dance in morning light.

With open arms, we greet the day,
Chasing clouds, we laugh and play.
Horizons stretch, our spirits fly,
Underneath this vast, blue sky.

Every journey starts with cheer,
In our hearts, the path is clear.
Grinning wide, we take each chance,
Rhapsody sings, we join the dance.

So let the world embrace our song,
In the melody, we all belong.
With laughter echoing afar,
Grinning horizons, our guiding star.

Echoes of Hope

In the quiet morn, we rise,
With dreams that touch the sky.
Whispers of a brighter day,
Together, we learn to fly.

Beneath the shadows, hearts ignite,
A flicker in the dark.
Each moment, a step toward light,
Guided by hope's spark.

Embracing every failure's tale,
With strength, we start anew.
Across the hills, our courage sails,
In faith, we'll break right through.

Through storms that rage, we stand so bold,
Hand in hand, we strive.
The story of our lives unfold,
With echoes that revive.

In the tapestry of dreams we weave,
Resilience shapes our fate.
With every breath, we firmly believe,
Hope stays, we captivate.

Melodies of Joyful Dreams

In fields of gold, we dance with grace,
The world a canvas bright.
Together, we find our sacred space,
Where melodies take flight.

With laughter ringing, spirits soar,
In every sweet refrain.
We paint our hopes forevermore,
In sunshine and in rain.

Awake to dreams that gently call,
Through valleys, we will roam.
Embracing warmth, we'll never fall,
In our hearts, we find home.

As stars align in endless night,
With joy our hearts embrace.
Each note a journey to the light,
Together, in this space.

With every heartbeat, love will sing,
Creating magic bright.
In melodies the world will bring,
Our dreams become the light.

Crescendo of Bright Horizons

The dawn awakens, colors blend,
A canvas bold and wide.
In the distance, dreams ascend,
On wings of hope, we ride.

With every heartbeat, new designs,
The future calls us near.
Embracing paths that intertwine,
We chase away all fear.

Through valleys deep and mountains tall,
We journey hand in hand.
With courage, we can face it all,
Together, we take a stand.

The music of the stars will play,
In harmony, we rise.
Beneath the light of a brand new day,
Our spirits touch the skies.

In every whisper, promise glows,
The horizon sings so bright.
As we become the hope that flows,
In journeys filled with light.

Harmonies of Laughter Unveiled

In gentle breezes, laughter sings,
A symphony of cheer.
With open hearts, we find our wings,
Together, year by year.

Each moment cherished, woven tight,
In joy, we find our way.
Embracing warmth, we set our sights,
On brighter, bolder days.

As echoes of our laughter play,
Like ripples on a stream.
Together, we'll chase clouds away,
And dance within a dream.

With smiles that light the darkest nights,
In unity, we stand.
Through every challenge, we take flight,
In harmony, hand in hand.

So let the world hear our delight,
With laughter, pure and free.
In every heart, the spark ignites,
Together, we shall be.

The Flourishing of Joyful Spirits

In gardens where laughter blooms,
The sunlight paints each gentle room.
With every smile that takes to flight,
The world reveals its pure delight.

Hearts dance to a cheerful tune,
Underneath the silver moon.
Each moment shines, a vibrant hue,
A symphony of joy anew.

Soft whispers breeze through the air,
Carrying hopes beyond compare.
In every glimmer of the night,
The spirit thrives, a radiant light.

Together we rise, hand in hand,
Painting dreams upon the sand.
With every beat, our hearts align,
In the flourishing, we intertwine.

So let us cherish every spark,
Guiding love through every dark.
For in this bond, we find our song,
A joyful spirit where we belong.

Arc of Upward Smiles

Along the path of fleeting time,
We lift our heads, our hearts a rhyme.
With every challenge, we embrace,
A brighter world, a boundless space.

Our laughter spreads like morning light,
Chasing shadows, bounding bright.
In every moment, we ascend,
On arcs of joy that never end.

The echoes of our joyous cries,
Are wings that lift us to the skies.
Each smile a spark, a shining beam,
Together weaving vibrant dreams.

Through valleys deep, on mountains high,
We chase the colors of the sky.
Hand in hand, with spirits wide,
In upward smiles, we will abide.

So let the world hear our refrain,
Of hope and love, our sweet campaign.
In every heart, a flame ignites,
An arc of smiles that always lights.

Serenade of Bright Intentions

With gentle notes, our hearts compose,
A serenade that softly flows.
In moments shared, intentions clear,
We craft a melody sincere.

Each word we speak a sweet embrace,
A guiding light in any space.
With harmony, our spirits soar,
Together strong, forevermore.

In every dream we dare to weave,
A tapestry of love we cleave.
With tender hopes like flowers bright,
We nurture joy with all our might.

In laughter shared and kindness spread,
A vibrant thread that weaved and led.
Together, we can change the world,
A serenade of hope unfurled.

As stars above begin to gleam,
We gather strength, fulfill our dream.
For every song we dare to sing,
Bring forth the joy that life can bring.

Echoes of Glowing Joy

In twilight's glow, our laughter rings,
Resounding where the heartache clings.
Each echo bounces, bright and clear,
A melody that we hold dear.

Across the hills, beneath the stars,
The music travels, near and far.
With every note, a promise plays,
Of glowing joy in endless ways.

We gather moments, soft and bright,
In whispered dreams that grace the night.
With every heartbeat, we unite,
Creating echoes of pure light.

The warmth of love in every glance,
Awakens hope, ignites the chance.
Together, we can chase the dawn,
In echoes bright, a love reborn.

So let us sing, both loud and clear,
In every voice, let joy appear.
For in this world, as life employs,
We'll find our bliss in glowing joys.

Bright Harmonies of Tomorrow

In a world where dreams unite,
Voices rise with pure delight.
Colors blend beneath the sun,
Together we will rise as one.

Every note a promise made,
In the light, we'll not be swayed.
Melodies of love will shine,
Guiding us, a path divine.

Harmony will weave its thread,
In our hearts, no fear or dread.
Building bridges, hand in hand,
Creating hope across the land.

With each chord, we pave the way,
For a brighter, bolder day.
Songs of joy will fill the air,
In every heart, love's vibrant flare.

Together we can reach the skies,
Chasing dreams that never die.
In this dance, we'll find our place,
Singing out with boundless grace.

The Lyrical Glow of Hope

In shadows deep, a light appears,
Whispers soft to calm our fears.
Through the night, we find our tune,
Guided gently by the moon.

Each verse tells of brighter days,
Painting skies with hopeful rays.
In every heart, a spark ignites,
Filling souls with warm delights.

With each word, the world we mend,
Creating paths that never end.
Together we will rise and soar,
Unlocking dreams, forevermore.

A symphony of voices blend,
In unity, we will transcend.
The lyrical glow leads the way,
To a brighter, brand new day.

So let us sing, in harmony,
A song of love, wild and free.
In every heart, the music thrives,
In this glow, our hope survives.

Fanfare of Agile Aspirations

With every step, we chase the dream,
Rising high like a flowing stream.
A fanfare rings through valleys wide,
In our hearts, there's nothing to hide.

Hope is the rhythm, wild and bright,
In our journey, we find our light.
Every moment another chance,
Together in this vibrant dance.

Through the storm, we take a stand,
Building futures, hand in hand.
Each aspiration sparks a flame,
Firing souls with passion's name.

The road ahead may twist and turn,
In our hearts, the fire will burn.
With each note, our spirits soar,
A fanfare echoes evermore.

We'll gather dreams like stars that shine,
In the darkness, our paths align.
Together strong, we'll break the mold,
With agile hearts, our dreams unfold.

Whispers of Bright Inspirations

In the quiet, whispers rise,
Sowing seeds beneath the skies.
Thoughts take flight, a gentle breeze,
Carrying dreams like autumn leaves.

In every heartbeat, new ideas,
Courage grows, dispelling fears.
With every thought, a spark ignites,
Guiding visions, shining lights.

Through the silence, voices call,
Inspiration, a gift for all.
Rise we shall, through darkest nights,
Finding beauty in our flights.

Each whisper holds a world unseen,
Painting hopes in every dream.
With open hearts, we take a stand,
Creating futures, hand in hand.

So let us gather, truth in sight,
Whispers guiding us to light.
In our journey, bright and bold,
Stories of inspiration unfold.

Notes of Promise on the Breeze

Whispers dance upon the air,
Softly carried, light and rare.
Every promise, fresh and bright,
Fills the heart with pure delight.

Leaves that rustle, songs they weave,
In the heart, hope takes its leave.
Gentle breezes, futures clear,
Guiding dreams that persevere.

Underneath the vast expanse,
Every soul deserves a chance.
In the stillness, love will find,
Wings of promise, intertwined.

Every sigh a step to take,
Gifts of courage, never shake.
On this path, the heart will soar,
Notes of promise, evermore.

Through the valleys, spirits rise,
Painting dreams in endless skies.
With each breath, we weave and trace,
Notes of hope in time and space.

Tapestry of Happy Endeavors

Threads of laughter, bright and bold,
Woven stories to be told.
Colors mingle, hearts entwine,
In this tapestry divine.

Tiny moments stitched with care,
Happiness woven everywhere.
Joyful echoes in the seams,
We create our brightest dreams.

Hand in hand, we dance along,
To the rhythm of our song.
Every stitch, a promise made,
In this joy, we won't degrade.

Together we will face the night,
With these threads, we know our light.
In each endeavor, love will grow,
A tapestry of endless flow.

Each new chapter, fresh and wide,
In unity, we shall abide.
With hearts open, we will care,
For this tapestry we share.

The Canvas of Joyful Yearning

Strokes of color, bright and free,
On this canvas, you and me.
Brushes dance with hopes unbound,
In this art, love can be found.

Every heartbeat paints a scene,
Moments captured, vivid green.
In the quiet, dreams take flight,
Guided by the stars at night.

A splash of gold for all we crave,
Waves of wonder, hearts so brave.
With each layer, stories flow,
The canvas speaks what we all know.

Joyful yearnings blend and twist,
In this artwork, love's sweet kiss.
Colors merge, our spirits rise,
Underneath these vast, wide skies.

Every breath, a line defined,
In this canvas, love is blind.
We create, our hearts will sing,
On this canvas, hear us ring.

Ballad of the Dreamers' Glimpse

In the stillness, dreams take flight,
Softly painted in twilight.
Every whisper holds a key,
Unlocking worlds for you and me.

Through the haze of morning light,
Visionaries, futures bright.
With each glance, horizons roam,
In our shadows, dreams find home.

Echoes of a distant tune,
Dancing 'neath the silver moon.
All the stars begin to weave,
Ballads sung for those who believe.

In the quiet, visions blend,
Threads of fate that never end.
With our hopes, we craft the scene,
Carving paths where we have been.

As the sun dips low and deep,
In our hearts, these dreams we keep.
Let us sing, our spirits bright,
Ballad of our shared delight.

Cadence of Bright Beginnings

In the morning light we rise,
New horizons greet our eyes.
With whispers soft and hearts aglow,
We step into the world below.

Each moment fresh, each chance anew,
We chase the dreams that feel so true.
Joy dances in the fragrant air,
Awakening a vibrant flare.

Together we will face the day,
Hand in hand, we find our way.
With laughter sweet, a song we'll sing,
The world awaits our blossoming.

Let the colors paint our fate,
Embracing love, we won't be late.
In every heartbeat, every sigh,
We find the courage to soar high.

With courage rooted in our souls,
We'll navigate through life's vast shoals.
As mornings break with golden rays,
We'll cherish all our brand new days.

Symphony of Radiant Dreams

Softly, under starlit skies,
The magic of our dreams will rise.
With every note, our hearts will blend,
Creating music without end.

In melodies both sweet and bright,
We weave our hopes with pure delight.
The symphony of life we play,
Guiding us through night and day.

Each harmony a whisper clear,
Resounds within, dispelling fear.
Our dreams are woven with the light,
Illuminating darkest night.

With every chord, we dare to fly,
Together reaching for the sky.
In rhythmic steps, we'll find our way,
A dance of dreams, come what may.

United in this vivid song,
Where every heartbeat sings along.
As notes entwine in boundless streams,
We'll brave the path of radiant dreams.

Echoes of Luminous Hearts

In the silence, hear the sounds,
Of luminous hearts that love surrounds.
With echoes soft, they play their part,
Entwined forever, heart to heart.

Through shadows deep and valleys wide,
We carry dreams where hope resides.
In every echo, truth will find,
The way to linger in our minds.

Through whispered vows, our spirits rise,
And sparkle like the starlit skies.
Each heartbeat sings a song of grace,
A dance of love in time and space.

Together, we embrace the light,
In every dark our love ignites.
The echoes guide us on our way,
A testament to every day.

With luminous hearts, we stand as one,
With every dawn, a chance to run.
As echoes linger, we'll depart,
Forever bound by love's own art.

The Dance of Hopeful Souls

In twilight's glow, we find our place,
Each step a dream, a soft embrace.
With rhythms sweet, our spirits soar,
In harmony, forevermore.

The dance ignites, igniting fire,
In every twirl, we feel desire.
With every laugh, our worries fade,
A symphony of joy is made.

As stars align in skies of blue,
The music plays, our hearts stay true.
With every leap, our hopes will grow,
In this dance, we'll never slow.

Together as the night unfolds,
We weave our dreams, like threads of gold.
The dance of souls, a timeless art,
Uniting every beating heart.

As dawn arrives, we'll greet the day,
With open arms, we'll find our way.
In every moment, every role,
We'll cherish this, our hopeful soul.

Notes of Infinite Possibilities

In the stillness of a dream,
A melody begins to rise.
Each note, a spark of hope,
Whispers of the endless skies.

With every chord we dare to play,
New paths unfold beneath our feet.
In harmony, our hearts align,
Creating magic, bittersweet.

The canvas wide, the colors blend,
With brushes dipped in daring grace.
Each stroke a tale, a journey penned,
A symphony we all embrace.

Together we will chase the light,
In shadows deep, we find our way.
With courage, joy will take its flight,
In notes of love that dare to stay.

So let the music fill the air,
A dance of voices, bold and free.
In every heart, a secret dare,
To find the dreams that are meant to be.

Heartstrings and Laughter's Crescendo

In laughter's embrace, we find our cheer,
Heartstrings strummed, a melody bright.
With every grin, we draw near,
Creating moments wrapped in light.

Together we weave our stories tight,
In playful whispers, secrets shared.
Each chuckle sparks a newfound flight,
Throughout the bonds we've always dared.

With time as our canvas, we paint the days,
Tales of joy etched deep in our souls.
In each symphony, laughter plays,
Binding us whole, making us whole.

So let us dance in the sun's warm glow,
With hearts entwined in this sweet song.
Through life's rhythms, we'll ebb and flow,
Forever together, where we belong.

In laughter's crescendo, our spirits soar,
Each note a promise, each hug a key.
With every heartbeat, we're rich in lore,
Together we thrive, eternally free.

Rhapsody of Joyful Endeavors

In the dawn of dreams we wake,
Chasing whispers of the sun.
Each step we take, a joyful break,
In the rhapsody, we have begun.

With open hearts, we greet the day,
In every moment, wonders grow.
Through paths of light, we laugh and play,
Together, we'll let our spirits flow.

Adventure calls, its voice so clear,
In ventures bold, we find our way.
With every laugh, we shed our fear,
In joyful endeavors, we choose to stay.

As stars above begin to gleam,
We share our hopes, our dreams aligned.
In every pulse, we feel the beam,
Of rhapsodies that fate designed.

So let us wander, hand in hand,
Through all the valleys, hills, and streams.
In joyful notes, together stand,
Creating life from shared heart dreams.

Tapestry of Shining Smiles

In the fabric of our days, we weave,
Threads of laughter, warm and bright.
With every smile, we choose to believe,
That hope resides in pure delight.

Patterns form in shades of joy,
Each twinkle tells a cherished tale.
In this tapestry, we'll not destroy,
But gather strength when shadows wail.

Through every stitch and gentle touch,
We create a world of endless grace.
In kindness shared, we've found so much,
In every heart, a sacred place.

So let us gather, friends so near,
In the loom of life, we'll find our style.
With every bond, we chase the fear,
Crafting love through our shining smiles.

Together, let's embrace the light,
In a tapestry that time will hold.
We'll stitch the stars in the quiet night,
In memories, our hearts unfold.

Rhythms of Playful Anticipation

In the light of dawn's embrace,
Children dance with hopes to chase.
Whispers of dreams soar in the air,
Time stands still, caught unaware.

Colors swirl in a gentle breeze,
Joyful hearts and laughter tease.
Each moment blossoms, fresh and bright,
As shadows fade with incoming light.

The sun peeks through, eager and shy,
Encouraging waves of laughter to fly.
With every leap and every spin,
The world unfolds where joys begin.

Steps taken with a carefree grace,
Finding magic in every place.
Echoes of giggles fill the scene,
In this realm where all are seen.

Together we weave the threads of fun,
Playing beneath the warming sun.
Life's canvas rich with color and cheer,
In rhythms of joy, we draw near.

The Chorus of Smiling Intentions

Underneath the starlit skies,
Hearts align where laughter lies.
Voices rise with pure delight,
A chorus sung throughout the night.

With every note, we share a dream,
Filling hearts with hope's bright gleam.
Hands held tight in unity's song,
Together in this place, we belong.

The melody flows, a gentle breeze,
Lifting spirits, putting minds at ease.
With every smile, intentions bloom,
Filling the world with love's sweet tune.

In this dance of souls entwined,
We're the echoes of the kind.
Through laughter and joy, we find our way,
Guided by the light of day.

As stars surround, our voices soar,
Creating harmony forevermore.
In every chord, a promise stays,
In the chorus of our days.

Lullabies of Laughter Unfolding

Softly rolling in the night,
Laughter sparkles, pure delight.
Gentle whispers, stories shared,
In their warmth, we all are cared.

Dreams awaken with a sigh,
Chasing clouds across the sky.
Sweet lullabies drift and flow,
Where the seeds of joy will grow.

Moonbeams dance on sleepy heads,
Guiding dreams to cozy beds.
In the night, joy intertwines,
As the heart with laughter shines.

Each giggle holds a tale to tell,
Casting spells where all is well.
In the rhythm of sleepy sounds,
Love envelops, safe and sound.

While the stars keep watch above,
We drift softly, cradled in love.
With lullabies that gently sing,
To the dreams tomorrow brings.

The Brightness of United Aspirations

Gathered here, our dreams ignite,
Underneath the morning light.
Voices rise in hopeful prayer,
Together, we can go anywhere.

Each vision shared, a spark ignites,
Illuminating future sights.
In unison our hearts take flight,
Chasing possibilities, bold and bright.

With open minds and steady hands,
We're forging paths through shifting sands.
Every challenge met with grace,
In this journey, we find our place.

Empowered by the dreams we hold,
Creating stories waiting to be told.
Together we shape our fateful course,
Guided by an unstoppable force.

With courage, we rise to meet new days,
In the brightness of hopeful ways.
Through our union, we shall thrive,
Together, we will come alive.

The Dance of Aspirational Grins

In the glow of hopeful eyes,
Dreams take flight like vibrant kites.
Every smile a silent song,
Together, they dance, where hearts belong.

Whispers of joy fill the air,
With every twirl, they softly share.
Fingers trace the paths of fate,
In their embrace, they celebrate.

Sparkling laughter, a sweet refrain,
Chasing shadows, dancing in the rain.
With every step, courage grows,
A symphony of love, like a rose.

In the tapestry of light and grace,
Aspirational grins paint every space.
Hearts align, a radiant glow,
In the dance of dreams, they surely know.

Together in dreams, united they stand,
With every careful, guiding hand.
Hopeful journeys unfold with ease,
In the dance of life, they find their peace.

Vibrations of Blissful Moments

In the hush of twilight's sighs,
Laughter echoes beneath the skies.
Tender whispers in evening's light,
Create a moment, pure and bright.

Colors blend in love's embrace,
Soft vibrations, filled with grace.
Each heartbeat counts, a rhythmic tune,
As joy blossoms, like flowers in June.

Waves of laughter, so warm and clear,
Wrap around hearts, drawing near.
Every glance ignites a spark,
In these blissful moments, they leave their mark.

With every breath, the world renews,
Painting skies in vibrant hues.
Time suspends in softest caress,
In vibrations of bliss, they find their rest.

Together they savor dreams that soar,
In every hug, they want for more.
This dance of life, they celebrate,
In blissful moments, they find their fate.

Harmonizing Bright Futures

In the dawn of a brand new day,
Hopeful hearts find their way.
Notes of promise fill the air,
Harmonizing futures, bright and fair.

With every choice, paths intertwine,
Every moment, a glimmer to shine.
In laughter and kindness, they grow,
Creating gardens where dreams can flow.

Each step forward, a dance of trust,
In unity, they rise, as they must.
With hands held tight, they face the world,
As dreams and wishes are unfurled.

In the symphony of their sweet refrain,
Resonates joy amidst the pain.
A tapestry woven with threads of gold,
In harmonizing futures, their story unfolds.

Together they build, brick by brick,
Dreaming of moments that time can't pick.
With every heartbeat, their spirits soar,
In bright futures, forevermore.

Overture to Radiant Dreams

In the silence before the show,
Whispers of hope begin to flow.
Stars align in a velvet sky,
An overture where dreams can fly.

With every note of gentle grace,
Possibilities bloom in this sacred space.
Fingers dance on keys of fate,
An invitation to celebrate.

With visions bright, they take the stage,
In the story of life, they turn the page.
Every heartbeat a rhythmic hymn,
In the overture, their spirits swim.

Colors swirl in vibrant hues,
The canvas of dreams glimmers and woos.
Each moment crafted with care,
In radiant dreams, they find their shares.

Together they leap, together they soar,
With every whisper, they want for more.
In this moment, forever it seems,
An overture to their radiant dreams.

Chord of Uplifting Moments

In the morning light, we rise anew,
With whispers of hope, the sky so blue.
Every heartbeat sings, a gentle tune,
As dreams take flight, like stars in June.

Moments intertwine, a dance so sweet,
With laughter that fills the air we greet.
Each note, a memory, bright and clear,
In every corner, joy draws near.

Hands held tight, we journey along,
Creating a symphony, forever strong.
In every glance, a bond we find,
A melody of love, gently defined.

Through winding paths, the echoes stay,
Guiding us forward, come what may.
In harmony, our spirits blend,
A song of life, that never ends.

With gratitude deep, we cherish each day,
In the chord of moments, we beautifully play.
With every laugh, with every tear,
In this uplifting path, we hold dear.

Radiance in Every Note

In twilight's glow, a soft refrain,
Where dreams take shape, releasing pain.
Each whisper glows like morning's sun,
A tapestry of joy is spun.

Through silver strands, the melodies flow,
Carving secrets only we know.
In every beat, the heart ignites,
Radiance swirling, pure delight.

With every strum, the shadows fade,
Guided by light, our fears evade.
In harmony's grasp, we find our way,
A vibrant dance, a lively play.

Notes of laughter, quilted and bright,
Wrap us in warmth, a blanket of light.
In every measure, courage blooms,
Creating a space where love resumes.

The world unfolds, in rhythm and rhyme,
Moments that glitter, defying time.
With every sound, our spirits soar,
Radiance in every note, we adore.

The Art of Glimmering Joy

In the quiet dusk, a spark ignites,
Glimmers of joy, serenade the nights.
With every heartbeat, a canvas bright,
Painting the world in hues of light.

Through whispers soft, the secrets sing,
The art of feeling, a treasured thing.
In every smile, a spark divine,
Binding our souls, your hand in mine.

With each sunrise, we chase the day,
Crafting our dreams in vibrant array.
Every moment, a chance to create,
A masterpiece woven, a glorious fate.

In laughter's embrace, our spirits blend,
Finding the echoes that never end.
Each note, a gem, in life's sweet choir,
The art of joy, our hearts inspire.

Beneath the stars, our hopes align,
Glimmers of dreams in perfect time.
In every heartbeat, the magic flows,
In the art of joy, our love grows.

Waves of Boundless Delight

In the depths of night, the waves arise,
Whispers of joy beneath the skies.
With every crash, a promise made,
In the ocean of love, never to fade.

The tides dance forward, a rhythmic sway,
Guiding our hearts along the way.
In each swell, the laughter flows,
Waves of delight, where happiness grows.

Through salty air, we hear the call,
A symphony that unites us all.
In every splash, adventures bloom,
Painting our world, erasing gloom.

As the moonlight bathes the sea so bright,
We ride the waves, igniting the night.
In every dip and every rise,
Boundless delight beneath the skies.

With every journey, together we sail,
Through stormy weather, through calm and gale.
In the heart of the ocean, love takes flight,
Waves of joy, our guiding light.

Cadence of Gleaming Dreams

In the stillness of the night,
Whispers of wishes take flight.
Stars awaken, shining bright,
Guiding souls with gentle light.

Every heartbeat sings a tune,
Echoes of the silver moon.
Glimmers dance in soft delight,
Painting skies with colors bright.

Hopes entwined in stardust beams,
Floating softly, like silent dreams.
In the silence, courage streams,
Awakening the heart that gleams.

Journey forth with light anew,
From shadows cast, emerge to view.
Breathe in visions, bold and true,
The path is clear, the dream is you.

In every step, a story shared,
Moments cherished, hearts laid bare.
The cadence plays, forever paired,
In gleaming dreams, our souls declare.

The Resonance of Joyful Hearts

In laughter's echo, spirits soar,
Every heartbeat opens doors.
Joyful whispers fill the air,
Resonating everywhere.

Songs of friendship, pure and bright,
Colors dancing, love's pure light.
Together, we will always stand,
Hand in hand, a merry band.

Through the trials, we won't break,
In unity, our hearts awake.
A symphony of hope we'll make,
With every tremor, every quake.

With every smile, a spark ignites,
A chain of warmth, in dark nights.
Resonance of love ignites,
A melody that hearts recite.

In gentle moments, we delight,
Finding peace in the moonlight.
Joyful hearts will guide us on,
In this song, we find our dawn.

Sonata of Hopeful Aspirations

In the dawn of every day,
Hope emerges, lighting the way.
With dreams as sweet as morning dew,
Together, we'll pursue what's true.

A symphony of hearts aligned,
Notes of courage, love entwined.
Every step, a note we play,
In this sonata, come what may.

Through the valleys, mountains high,
With aspirations that touch the sky.
We rise, we fall, yet still we sing,
In hope's embrace, our spirits cling.

With every challenge, we grow strong,
Striking chords to our own song.
For in unity, our dreams unite,
An opus crafted in shared light.

In twilight's glow, we find our way,
Through shadows cast, we won't delay.
Together, in harmony's grace,
We'll write our dreams, our steadfast place.

Chorus of Glowing Visions

In the evening's soft embrace,
Visions glow, a warm trace.
Choruses of dreams unfold,
Stories whispered, secrets told.

Every star, a glimmering tale,
Guiding ships through night's pale sail.
With every breath, a vision born,
In the chorus, we are reborn.

Through the echoes of the past,
Glimmering futures, shadows cast.
Hope unites us, hand in hand,
In glowing visions, we will stand.

A melody of light we create,
With every step, we celebrate.
Chasing horizons, dreams in flight,
In our hearts, there burns a light.

Together we'll sing, together we'll soar,
In this chorus, forevermore.
Glowing visions, warm and bright,
Illuminate our journey's night.

Dance of Illuminated Visions

In twilight dreams, the shadows sway,
Beneath the stars, they find their way.
Colors blend, a vibrant sight,
In the night, all hearts take flight.

With each step, the visions bloom,
In rhythmic pulse, dispelling gloom.
Whispers of hope hover near,
Guiding souls with laughter and cheer.

Moonlit pathways light the ground,
As spirits rise, the joy unbound.
In unity, we dance as one,
Under the gaze of the silver sun.

Moments captured, fleeting, brief,
In every twirl, we find belief.
Illuminated by our dreams,
Together, nothing's as it seems.

Hold me close, let time stand still,
The echoes linger, a timeless thrill.
In this waltz of radiant grace,
We find our strength, we find our place.

Whispers of Radiant Futures

In dawn's embrace, new hopes arise,
A tapestry of endless skies.
Each whisper soft, a guiding light,
Leading us from dark to bright.

Visions painted with vibrant hues,
In every heart, a path to choose.
Dreams ignite, like stars in flight,
Embracing all, with pure delight.

Tomorrow calls with gentle hands,
A world awaits, where love expands.
Together we sow seeds of grace,
In every smile, a warm embrace.

Echoes fade but never die,
In whispered secrets, we can fly.
Radiant futures beckon near,
In unity, we cast out fear.

With every breath, let's forge ahead,
On paths of gold, by courage led.
For every dream that we ignite,
Will blossom in the morning light.

Dance of Illuminated Visions

In twilight dreams, the shadows sway,
Beneath the stars, they find their way.
Colors blend, a vibrant sight,
In the night, all hearts take flight.

With each step, the visions bloom,
In rhythmic pulse, dispelling gloom.
Whispers of hope hover near,
Guiding souls with laughter and cheer.

Moonlit pathways light the ground,
As spirits rise, the joy unbound.
In unity, we dance as one,
Under the gaze of the silver sun.

Moments captured, fleeting, brief,
In every twirl, we find belief.
Illuminated by our dreams,
Together, nothing's as it seems.

Hold me close, let time stand still,
The echoes linger, a timeless thrill.
In this waltz of radiant grace,
We find our strength, we find our place.

Whispers of Radiant Futures

In dawn's embrace, new hopes arise,
A tapestry of endless skies.
Each whisper soft, a guiding light,
Leading us from dark to bright.

Visions painted with vibrant hues,
In every heart, a path to choose.
Dreams ignite, like stars in flight,
Embracing all, with pure delight.

Tomorrow calls with gentle hands,
A world awaits, where love expands.
Together we sow seeds of grace,
In every smile, a warm embrace.

Echoes fade but never die,
In whispered secrets, we can fly.
Radiant futures beckon near,
In unity, we cast out fear.

With every breath, let's forge ahead,
On paths of gold, by courage led.
For every dream that we ignite,
Will blossom in the morning light.

Serenade of Shimmering Aspirations

A melody drifts on the breeze,
Carried softly through the trees.
Hopes awaken in the night,
Every star a dream in flight.

With harmonies that touch the soul,
Shimmering visions make us whole.
In the stillness, whispers soar,
A serenade forevermore.

Each note holds a trembling wish,
A longing wrapped in silken bliss.
In the concert of our days,
We find the strength in different ways.

Hope and courage intertwine,
As we chase what feels divine.
In every chord, a spark ignites,
Lighting paths through shadowed nights.

Together we will rise and sing,
Of all the joy that dreams can bring.
In this song of aspirations clear,
We draw the future ever near.

The Music of Unbroken Spirits

A rhythm pulses through the air,
In every heart, a flame laid bare.
Unbroken spirits, fierce and bold,
In notes of warmth, their stories told.

From distant lands, the echoes call,
A symphony that binds us all.
With every beat, we rise anew,
Our hearts unite in shades of blue.

With strength unyielding, we will stand,
A chorus forged, hand in hand.
In trials faced, our voices blend,
Each melody a steadfast friend.

Let sorrows drift like autumn leaves,
In harmony, there's love that cleaves.
Through storms of doubt, we'll find our way,
With music's light to guide the day.

Together we'll create the sound,
Of spirits free, forever found.
In every note, we leave a spark,
A legacy that lights the dark.

Glittering Notes of Delight

In the moonlight's tender glow,
Laughter dances, soft and slow.
Stars twinkle in the velvet night,
Whispers echo, pure delight.

Melodies flit through the air,
Carrying love, free from despair.
Hearts entwined in gentle cheer,
Every moment, magic near.

A symphony of joyful sights,
Colors weave in dazzling flights.
Like fireflies in the deep dark,
Each spark ignites a vibrant spark.

Together we sing, side by side,
In this bliss, we take our stride.
With each note, our spirits rise,
Reaching up towards the skies.

In this embrace of sweet embrace,
Life's treasures, a warm space.
Glittering notes of pure delight,
Our hearts dance through the night.

Joy's Melodic Journey

Across the hills, the music flows,
Carrying dreams where sunlight glows.
With every step, the rhythm beats,
Joy's journey, where heart and soul meets.

Through fields of gold, we wander free,
Nature's song, a symphony.
Soft whispers in the warm spring air,
Chasing worries, stripped bare.

Each laugh shared like a precious gem,
Moments cherished, a diadem.
With joyful hearts, we rise above,
In harmony, we find our love.

As melodies shift and intertwine,
The essence of joy, so divine.
In every pause, we feel alive,
In this journey, we thrive.

When twilight falls, our spirits soar,
Echoes of laughter, forevermore.
With joy's melody, we unite,
A voyage of pure delight.

The Chorus of Vibrant Aspirations

In the horizon, dreams emerge,
Voices rise, a hopeful surge.
Across the skies, ambitions bloom,
A chorus strong, dispelling gloom.

Each note sung with passion bright,
Illuminated by our shared light.
Together we stand, hearts ablaze,
In vibrant hopes, we shall amaze.

Through valleys low and mountains high,
Our aspirations reach the sky.
Unified, we chase the dawn,
With every tear, our fears are gone.

As we climb, the world will see,
The strength that lies in unity.
A melody of vibrant dreams,
Flowing in cascading streams.

Let the chorus serenade,
A soundtrack for the plans we've made.
With every voice, we spark the fire,
In this journey, we aspire.

Harmonizing Infinite Dreams

In a tapestry woven with care,
Dreams unfurl like petals rare.
Each thread sings a tale untold,
In harmonies, our hopes unfold.

With every heart as one, we rise,
Echoes of love in starry skies.
Infinite possibilities gleam,
As we dance through life's great dream.

Notes of courage, whispers of grace,
Together we find our rightful place.
With open minds, we chase the light,
In this symphony of insight.

Let the world hear our embrace,
In every struggle, we find our pace.
Harmonizing dreams, we ignite,
In perfect synchrony, taking flight.

Through valleys of shadows, we'll tread,
With love as our compass, we're led.
In the symphony, we are whole,
Infinite dreams, one shared soul.

Fanfare of Bright Tomorrows

In dawn's embrace we rise anew,
With colors bold and skies so blue.
The dreams we chase will light our way,
As stars align to greet the day.

With every heartbeat, hopes ignite,
A symphony of pure delight.
The whispers of the future call,
Together we will stand, not fall.

Through every challenge, hand in hand,
We'll weave our tales upon the land.
In courage dressed, we march ahead,
A fanfare sung for dreams widespread.

Embrace the joy in every stride,
With laughter echoing deep inside.
The sun will rise, the shadows flee,
In bright tomorrows, we will be.

With hope like seeds in fertile ground,
We'll sow our visions all around.
A harvest rich, with love we'll share,
In unity, we breathe the air.

The Light in Every Melody

In whispers soft, the music plays,
A gentle tune in myriad ways.
Each note a spark, a guiding flame,
The heart remembers every name.

From echoes past to future dreams,
In every chord, hope brightly gleams.
With every beat, we find our song,
Together, where we all belong.

The light within each melody,
Unlocks the door to harmony.
In laughter shared and tears shed warm,
We dance through life, through every storm.

Let music lift our spirits high,
And paint the world with colors nigh.
In symphonies that intertwine,
The light of love, forever shine.

Through every note, a story told,
In rhythms rich, we are consoled.
Together, let our hearts entwine,
In every melody, we find.

Flourish of Hopeful Echoes

In gardens where the wildflowers bloom,
Hope flutters softly, dispelling gloom.
Each petal whispers dreams of grace,
In every heart, a sacred space.

With gentle winds, our spirits soar,
In echoes rich, we long for more.
The laughter shared, the stories spun,
Together in the golden sun.

Through valleys deep and mountains high,
The veils of doubt begin to fly.
In every tear, a seed is sown,
To flourish bright, we are not alone.

The dance of shadows, the light we crave,
In every challenge, we are brave.
With arms wide open, let love guide,
In hopeful echoes, we abide.

To nurture dreams that gently rise,
In every soul, the future lies.
Through time and space, we will ignite,
A flourish bright, a shared delight.

Quickstep of Illuminated Paths

In twilight's glow, our journey starts,
A quickstep dance of hopeful hearts.
We weave through shadows, find the light,
And step with grace into the night.

With every stride, we break the chains,
In unity, our love remains.
Through whispered winds, adventure calls,
Illuminated paths, our spirits enthrall.

The stars above, they guide our way,
With dreams alive in bright display.
Each moment cherished, vibrant, true,
In every heartbeat, life anew.

Through laughter bright and trials faced,
We journey forth, our fears erased.
With every step, we learn to flow,
In dance of life, our spirits grow.

So take my hand, let's soar together,
Through every storm and sunny weather.
In quickstep rhythm, bold and free,
Illuminated paths await you and me.

Blissful Cadence of Hope

In the quiet morn, dreams arise,
Whispers of light touch the skies.
Hearts beat softly, a gentle song,
Guiding us forward, where we belong.

Through the trials, we find our way,
With every dawn, a brand new day.
Hope dances lightly upon the breeze,
Filling our souls, putting us at ease.

In laughter shared, moments align,
The beauty of now, a treasure divine.
Together we rise, hand in hand,
Building a future, a promised land.

As shadows fade, colors ignite,
Painting our path, bold and bright.
In the symphony of life, we play,
Creating our story, come what may.

So let us embrace, each chance bestowed,
With a heart full of dreams, let love explode.
In the cadence of hope, we find our song,
In this blissful dance, we all belong.

Trills of Radiant Possibilities

A gentle breeze stirs the leaves,
With the promise of more than it receives.
Every note a spark in the air,
Whispering secrets beyond compare.

In the dance of time, we sway and twirl,
Unlocking wonders as dreams unfurl.
With eyes wide open, we see so clear,
The trills of hope drawing us near.

Challenges rise like clouds overhead,
But with courage and grace, we forge ahead.
Every stumble brings wisdom's grace,
In this journey we find our place.

Filling the world with vibrant hues,
A tapestry woven of countless views.
In every heartbeat, we rise anew,
Chasing the dreams that we hold true.

So let us sing of the paths we create,
Of radiant futures that patiently wait.
In each trilling note, possibilities shine,
A melody sweet, forever divine.

The Joyful Chorus of Tomorrow

In the dawn's embrace, hearts collide,
With hope and dreams, our spirits glide.
The laughter of children fills the air,
With innocent joy, free from care.

Every sunrise brings promise anew,
A canvas of colors, a vibrant view.
Together we sing, voices unite,
In the joyful chorus, hearts take flight.

Through mountains high and valleys low,
We journey together, letting love flow.
With each note sung, we rise above,
Filling the world with boundless love.

In shadows cast, we'll find our light,
Guiding each other through the night.
With each step forward, courage grows,
In this symphony, warmth overflows.

So let us dance to the rhythm of fate,
Seizing the moments, before it's too late.
In tomorrow's embrace, we shall soar,
In the joyful chorus, forevermore.

Explorations of Shining Possibilities

With stars as guides, we sail the seas,
In the heart's compass, we find the keys.
Each wave whispers tales of the bold,
Adventures waiting to be told.

In questing spirits, we chase the light,
Unraveling mysteries, chasing delight.
The horizon beckons, a magic lure,
Each step we take opens a door.

Through valleys deep and mountains grand,
We weave our dreams with an open hand.
Every sunrise a canvas, fresh and wide,
In explorations, we take the ride.

With laughter and love as our guide,
Together we roam, hearts open wide.
In the vast expanse, together we stand,
Finding our way through a wondrous land.

So let us journey, eyes shining bright,
In search of the magic that feels just right.
In exploration's embrace, we find our way,
Shining possibilities brighten the day.

The Rhythm of Future Radiance

In dawn's embrace, the colors blend,
A symphony of light, we comprehend.
Dreams take flight on gentle breeze,
With every heartbeat, time's sweet tease.

Hope arises like the morning sun,
Each moment cherished, battles won.
Whispers of fate guide our way,
In the rhythm of night turning to day.

Through valleys deep and mountains high,
We dance to tunes that lift us nigh.
The future glows, a canvas pure,
With every step, we find our cure.

Bright visions pulse in the stark night air,
Together we rise, chasing despair.
As stars align, our spirits soar,
In the rhythm of future, we adore.

Hand in hand, we forge our path,
In unity, we harness the math.
The world awakens, our hearts ignite,
In this radiant rhythm, we take flight.

Joyful Measures of Aspiration

With every note, our spirits lift,
In joyful measures, a precious gift.
We weave our dreams in melodies bright,
Chasing the shadows, seeking the light.

Boundless zeal in every song,
A chorus of hope where we belong.
Each step forward, a dance of chance,
In the music of life, we joyously prance.

The echoes of laughter fill the air,
In moments shared, we conquer despair.
With every heartbeat, our spirits align,
In joyful measures, the stars brightly shine.

We sing of dreams that know no end,
In this symphony, hearts we mend.
Together we strive, hand in hand,
With joyful measures, we take our stand.

Beyond the horizon, adventures await,
In the rhythm of hope, we celebrate.
With every breath, our wishes take flight,
In joyful measures, we embrace the night.

Starry Notes of Elevated Spirits

Under the canvas of a celestial dome,
We find our hearts, our spirits roam.
Starry notes whisper in the night,
Guiding our dreams to take their flight.

In the silence, magic hums,
Flowing like rivers, the wonder comes.
Every twinkle, a tale to share,
A tapestry woven with tender care.

Elevated spirits soar above,
In the dance of stars, we find our love.
Every heartbeat mirrors the glow,
Of starry notes that ebb and flow.

With hopes ignited in the cool night,
We gather dreams, our future bright.
In the cosmos' embrace, we unite,
In starry notes, our spirits ignite.

Together we journey, hand in hand,
On the path of starlight, we understand.
Lives intertwined, like constellations' art,
In starry notes, we share one heart.

The Sonnet of Glowing Possibilities

In the quiet hush of breaking dawn,
Where dreams awaken, and fears are gone.
A sonnet woven with threads of gold,
In the tapestry of life, stories told.

Every heartbeat a chance to grow,
In possibilities, our spirits glow.
With every sigh, the universe sings,
Of hopes and wishes that freedom brings.

We dance in the light of endless skies,
With faith like anchors, we shall rise.
In the garden of dreams, we sow our seeds,
Nurtured by love, fulfilling our needs.

With every whisper of the gentle breeze,
We embrace the future, discovering ease.
A sonnet of life, where hearts collide,
In glowing possibilities, we confide.

As the sun sets on another day,
We treasure moments that softly sway.
Together we shine, in unity's bliss,
In the sonnet of glowing, we find our kiss.

Serenade of Sunlit Faces

In the morning glow, we rise,
With laughter bright, we touch the skies.
Each sunbeam hugs the world so tight,
Painting dreams in golden light.

Joyful whispers fill the air,
Together, hearts dance without a care.
In this moment, we find our place,
A melody of sunlit grace.

Through fields of flowers, we will roam,
Hand in hand, we make our home.
The sun above, our guiding star,
In this journey, we've come so far.

With every step, we walk in hope,
In harmony, we learn to cope.
The serenade, a sweet embrace,
Forevermore, sunlit faces.

As twilight whispers softly near,
We cherish laughter, shed each tear.
For in this song, we know it's true,
The sunlit faces shine anew.

Crescendo of Bright Beginnings

Awakening to morning's cheer,
Each dawn we rise, our vision clear.
With open hearts, we greet the day,
In the light, we find our way.

A symphony of hopes we sing,
With every note, we start to wing.
Together, we create the sound,
In this moment, joy is found.

The colors burst, a vivid show,
In every step, our spirits grow.
Celebrating life, we take our stand,
Side by side, hand in hand.

With dreams that soar like birds in flight,
We chase the stars that shine so bright.
A crescendo that lifts us high,
In our hearts, we learn to fly.

Tomorrow waits with open arms,
New journeys filled with endless charms.
In every breath, we sing along,
A symphony of love, our song.

Chasing the Light of Tomorrow

The horizon calls, we set our gaze,
With a fire within, setting hearts ablaze.
Every step forward, leaving the past,
In the chase for tomorrow, we hold steadfast.

Whispers of dreams float through the night,
Guiding our hopes, making shadows light.
Through valleys deep and mountains tall,
In each struggle, we learn to stand tall.

With stars above as our guiding light,
We embrace the unknown, banishing fright.
Chasing the dawn with courage so pure,
In the echoes of hope, we stand assured.

As the sun breaks through, brightening the skies,
We dance with joy, letting laughter rise.
Each moment cherished, a treasure to find,
In the light of tomorrow, we leave fears behind.

Together we wander, hand in hand,
Crafting our path, a dream so grand.
In the chase for tomorrow, our spirits shall soar,
With hearts wide open, we seek and explore.

The Dance of Optimistic Hearts

In the rhythm of life, we sway,
With every beat, come what may.
Optimistic hearts in a joyful trance,
Lost in the magic, we take our chance.

Through every challenge, we find our way,
With hope as our guide, we won't dismay.
Together we stand, for each other we fight,
In the dance of dreams, we shine so bright.

With laughter that echoes, we fill the air,
The dance of our spirits, light as a prayer.
In circles of friendship, our worries fade,
In this celebration, our love is displayed.

As the stars twinkle and the moonlight glows,
Our optimistic hearts will always know.
In the dance of tomorrow, we twirl with grace,
Embracing the journey, our rightful place.

So let the music play, let kindness impart,
For we are the dreamers, the optimistic heart.
Together we flow in this beautiful dance,
Chasing our dreams, in love's sweet romance.

The Dance of Unfolding Joy

In the morning light we sway,
Hearts invite the warmth of play.
Every step a blissful sign,
Whispers sweet, our souls entwine.

Fields of laughter greet the day,
Grounded in the bright bouquet.
Each twirl ignites a spark within,
A joyful song, where we begin.

With every leap, the world expands,
Footprints drawn on golden sands.
Together we embrace the rise,
A dance beneath the open skies.

Let the rhythm guide the way,
Joyful spirits here to stay.
In the swirling breeze we find,
A dance of heart, a joyful mind.

As the sun dips low and slows,
The laughter fades, the stillness grows.
Yet in our hearts, forever bright,
The dance continues through the night.

Waves of Unyielding Smiles

Gentle whispers kiss the shore,
Laughter echoes evermore.
Each wave rolls with a sweet embrace,
A tapestry of joy and grace.

Sunset paints the sky ablaze,
In its warmth, we bask and gaze.
Smiles rise like foam on seas,
Carried forth by playful breeze.

Footprints dancing in the sand,
Memories crafted, hand in hand.
In every crest, in every fall,
We find the beauty, we find it all.

Ripples of joy that never cease,
In sharing moments, find our peace.
Each swell a promise, strong and true,
Waves of smiles, forever new.

As twilight hugs the ocean's edge,
Adventure lingers, a gentle pledge.
With laughter in our hearts, we roam,
Together in this, we are home.

The Dance of Unfolding Joy

In the morning light we sway,
Hearts invite the warmth of play.
Every step a blissful sign,
Whispers sweet, our souls entwine.

Fields of laughter greet the day,
Grounded in the bright bouquet.
Each twirl ignites a spark within,
A joyful song, where we begin.

With every leap, the world expands,
Footprints drawn on golden sands.
Together we embrace the rise,
A dance beneath the open skies.

Let the rhythm guide the way,
Joyful spirits here to stay.
In the swirling breeze we find,
A dance of heart, a joyful mind.

As the sun dips low and slows,
The laughter fades, the stillness grows.
Yet in our hearts, forever bright,
The dance continues through the night.

Waves of Unyielding Smiles

Gentle whispers kiss the shore,
Laughter echoes evermore.
Each wave rolls with a sweet embrace,
A tapestry of joy and grace.

Sunset paints the sky ablaze,
In its warmth, we bask and gaze.
Smiles rise like foam on seas,
Carried forth by playful breeze.

Footprints dancing in the sand,
Memories crafted, hand in hand.
In every crest, in every fall,
We find the beauty, we find it all.

Ripples of joy that never cease,
In sharing moments, find our peace.
Each swell a promise, strong and true,
Waves of smiles, forever new.

As twilight hugs the ocean's edge,
Adventure lingers, a gentle pledge.
With laughter in our hearts, we roam,
Together in this, we are home.

A Harmony of Bright Possibilities

Underneath the starlit skies,
Dreams awaken, hope resides.
Notes of laughter fill the air,
In this harmony, we share.

Colors blend in twilight's hue,
Every moment feels brand new.
A symphony of shining hearts,
In each embrace, a world departs.

Voices rise in sweet refrain,
Unity within the rain.
Together we will paint the night,
In strokes of love, in beams of light.

Every whisper, every song,
Helps us feel we all belong.
In this symphony, we soar,
A harmony that opens doors.

As dawn awakens, bright and clear,
Possibilities draw near.
In the light, our spirits sing,
Together, joy is everything.

Melodies of Lively Dreams

In the hush of twilight gleam,
Lively dance, with hopes we dream.
Each note a whisper, soft and free,
Carried on the breeze, we see.

Stars like diamonds in the night,
Guide our hearts to pure delight.
With a rhythm of our own,
Blissfully, we have grown.

Every heartbeat, every sigh,
Echoes in the velvet sky.
A chorus formed of tender beams,
In the melodies of dreams.

Chasing shadows, we create,
A masterpiece, we celebrate.
In every step, in every turn,
A passion bright, a flame that burns.

As dawn breaks, the song remains,
Filling life with sweet refrains.
In the tapestry of our seams,
We find the joy in lively dreams.

Sway of Joyous Endeavors

In fields of gold we dance with glee,
Our laughter echoes, wild and free.
With every step, our spirits rise,
We chase the sun beneath bright skies.

Each moment sings a vibrant tune,
As dreams take flight, like stars in June.
Together we embrace the night,
Our hearts aflame, a pure delight.

In gentle winds, we find our way,
Through trials faced, we dare to stay.
With hope as guide, we tread the path,
And spark the joy, ignite the wrath.

A tapestry of hearts entwined,
In love's embrace, our souls aligned.
We share the burdens, share the cheer,
In unity, we conquer fear.

So let us sway in this sweet dance,
With joyous hearts, we take our chance.
As life unfolds, we'll keep the pace,
In every challenge, find our grace.

Laughter's Gentle Serenade

A melody drifts through the air,
With every giggle, burdens rare.
In joyful moments, time stands still,
As laughter warms, it starts to fill.

The heart's a drum, it beats in time,
In harmony, we craft our rhyme.
With friends around, our spirits soar,
Each chuckle shared, we long for more.

In starlit nights, we'll reminisce,
Of silly jokes and moments missed.
The world aglow with smiles and cheer,
In laughter's arms, we have no fear.

Through ups and downs, we find the light,
In playful jests, the world feels right.
A dance of joy, both bold and free,
In laughter's serenade, we see.

So let us gather, share a tale,
With laughter leading, we shall sail.
In this sweet song, our hearts unite,
A gentle serenade, pure delight.

The Heartbeat of Bright Possibilities

In whispered dreams, the future calls,
A rhythm pulses, as hope enthralls.
With every heartbeat, courage grows,
In unseen paths, life gently flows.

With open eyes, we greet the dawn,
In colors bright, the past is gone.
Embracing change, we weave our fate,
With hearts aflame, we learn to wait.

Each step we take, a world to find,
In every moment, love's aligned.
With faith as guide, potential shines,
In the heart's beat, our future twines.

In shared dreams, our spirits soar,
Unlocking doors, we yearn for more.
Adventure calls, it dares us on,
To tread the path 'til break of dawn.

So fear not change, for life's a song,
In vibrant notes, where we belong.
With every breath, a chance we see,
The heartbeat whispers, "You're meant to be."

Symphony of Shining Spirits

In symphonies of joy, we rise,
With shining spirits, reach the skies.
Together, we compose our song,
In harmony, where hearts belong.

With every note that softly plays,
We find the beauty in our days.
In laughter's dance, our souls ignite,
As dreams take flight, and hearts feel light.

Through trials faced, we find the tune,
In darkest nights, we'll find the moon.
With hands held tight, we share the sound,
In unity, our voices found.

The symphony of life unfolds,
With tales of love and strength retold.
With every chord, our spirits shine,
In this great orchestra, you are mine.

So let us play, and let love lead,
In every moment, plant a seed.
As shining spirits, we will sway,
In symphony, we find our way.

Whispers of Radiant Dreams

In twilight's embrace, dreams softly bloom,
Whispers of hope in the silvery gloom.
Stars dance above with a shimmering gleam,
Lighting the paths of each radiant dream.

Petals of laughter brush against the night,
Carried by breezes that shimmer with light.
Each moment unfolds like a delicate thread,
Woven with magic where dreams have been led.

A symphony played on a harp of the skies,
Echoing gently as the old story flies.
Footsteps of starlight trace patterns anew,
Leading the way to a world bright and true.

In quiet reflection, the heart finds its beat,
Dancing on clouds with a soft, steady heat.
The whispers remind us we're never alone,
As radiant dreams weave a tapestry home.

With every heartbeat, our hopes intertwine,
Breathing life into the dreams that are mine.
In the night's warm embrace, let us finally rise,
To dance with the stars far beyond earthly ties.

Melodies of Laughter Beneath the Stars

Under a canopy stitched with bright light,
We gather together, hearts taking flight.
Laughter unfolds like the wings of a bird,
As melodies soar with each whispers heard.

In that soft space where the shadows reside,
Stories unfold, like a jubilant tide.
Each note that we share, brilliantly free,
Ties us together like roots of a tree.

Beneath the vast heavens, we dance and we sing,
Embracing the joy that the sweet moments bring.
With every chuckle, the stars seem to smile,
Transforming the night, making our world worthwhile.

In the glow of the moon, our worries take flight,
Floating like feathers on a blanket of light.
Each giggle and whisper a gift to the night,
As we weave our dreams with the cosmos in sight.

So let us rejoice in this timeless delight,
For memories linger in the warmth of the night.
With laughter as music, we'll dance through the years,
Creating a bond that forever endears.

Harmonies of Hope in Bloom

In gardens where whispers of springtime arise,
Blooms of hope glisten, painting the skies.
Every petal unfurls with a promise anew,
In harmonies sweet that the heart will pursue.

The dew on the leaves sings a soft lullaby,
As breezes caress, making spirits comply.
With each rising sun, the dreams gently wake,
Embracing the world for a new life to take.

Colors blend slowly in a grand bouquet,
Telling our stories, as night turns to day.
With every heartbeat, the symphony grows,
Filling the air with compassion it knows.

In moments of quiet, the seeds start to sprout,
Filling our souls with what life's all about.
From shadows of doubt, the bloom does survive,
Carrying whispers of hope, alive.

As petals drift gently on morning's soft breeze,
We gather the courage, embracing with ease.
In harmonies woven, our futures shall gleam,
For hope, like a flower, forever shall beam.

Echoes of Joyful Aspirations

In the quiet dawn, where the light starts to creep,
Aspirations rise from the dreams that we keep.
Whispers of courage fill the cool morning air,
As echoes of joy dance, floating everywhere.

Each step that we take is a journey of heart,
Crafting the story where all of us start.
With laughter and love, we soar to the skies,
With wings built of wishes that refuse to disguise.

In the tapestry woven with threads of delight,
Every color tells of our hopes shining bright.
The rhythm of passion ignites with each day,
As echoes of kindness gently find their way.

Through valleys of doubt, through mountains we climb,
Together we rise, transcending all time.
With every heartbeat, we find our own way,
In echoes of joy that refuse to decay.

In horizons unveiled, our dreams blend and sway,
Carried by passion in the light of the day.
Each aspiration a lantern that beams,
Guiding our spirits to follow our dreams.

www.ingramcontent.com/pod-product-compliance
Ingram Content Group UK Ltd.
Pitfield, Milton Keynes, MK11 3LW, UK
UKHW020051171224
452675UK00013B/1061